Joannie Rochette

Canadian Ice Princess

Second Edition

CREATIVE MEDIA, INC.
PO Box 6270
Whittier, California 90609-6270
United States of America

www.CreativeMedia.net

Front cover photo by J. Barry Mittan; back cover photo by Jay Adeff
Cover and Book design by Joseph Dzidrums
Copy Editor: Elizabeth Allison

First Edition: January 2010
Second Edition: March 2010

Library of Congress Control Number: 2010903265

ISBN 978-0-9826435-0-1   10 9 8 7 6 5 4 3 2

Joannie Rochette

Canadian Ice Princess

Second Edition

An Unauthorized Biography by

Christine Dzidrums *and* **Leah Rendon**

Creative Media Publishing

We are grateful to the following people for their help.
Without their support this book wouldn't exist.

Jay Adeff

Elizabeth Allison

Joseph Dzidrums

Joshua Dzidrums

J. Barry Mittan

Mom and Dad

Contents

1

"The Drive for Five"

On the afternoon of the long program at the 2009 Canadian Figure Skating Championships, Joannie Rochette paced backstage as she waited to take the ice.

In her bid to win a fifth straight Canadian title, Joannie had lost her focus during the short program. She now sat in second place, trailing leader Cynthia Phaneuf.

Joannie's nerves jangled. Her mind raced. Her adrenalin pumped. Her hands shook. She loved every minute of it.

Joannie thrived on her reputation as a comeback queen. She loved surprising people after they counted her out.

Manon Perron stood supportively by Joannie's side as she had for so many years. She was not just her coach – she was a friend and a second mother. Manon leaned into Joannie's ear and reminded her that she was well-trained for this competition. She could rely on muscle memory to skate a strong performance.

Joannie closed her eyes and visualized her program. In her mind she landed every jump securely. Joannie opened her eyes. She felt ready.

Joannie and Manon walked past a row of cameras and stood by the rink boards. The crowd in the large arena murmured excitedly when they caught sight of their champion. Joannie removed her skate guards and glided onto the ice. She looked into Manon's eyes.

"Another moment of truth for our champion," four-time world champion Kurt Browning, who worked for the Canadian television network CBC, told the TV viewing audience.

Joannie bent down to adjust her skates' laces.

"Ladies and gentlemen, now representing Quebec, please welcome Joannie Rochette!"

Joannie and Manon exchanged their traditional good luck hand slaps. The crowd cheered loudly for the Canadian champion as her coach gave her a last minute pep talk.

"This is a big moment," the CBC commentator remarked.

Joannie skated to center ice and assumed her role as a Spanish dancer. She looked determined and focused. The familiar sounds of Joannie's music, "Concierto de Aranjuez," filled the air. Suddenly she felt calm and relaxed. Joannie no longer worried about her troubles in the short program. She vowed to surrender her heart to her extraordinary long program.

Joannie skated assertively into her first jump combination, the triple Lutz-double toe-double loop, and landed it with ease. Then she hit a clean triple flip and a big triple loop. When Joannie flew into her elegant combination spin, the crowd roared with approval.

Before the audience could finish applauding, Joannie landed another triple Lutz. Then she hit a very impressive triple-triple sequence. As she began her difficult footwork section, the crowd cheered with gusto. Joannie floated across the ice with the grace of a ballerina and the power of a world-class athlete. Then she flew into a double Axel followed by another double Axel!

Joannie continued attacking her routine. She launched into the air, turned three times and came down confidently on her blade to land her seventh triple jump. The crowd rose from their seats before her routine even ended. She could barely hear her music over the audience's cheers. When the music's last note played, she placed her hands over her face and pumped her arms in victory.

"Four short minutes," the CBC commentator raved. "But they speak volumes about what a great champion has to offer."

"The drive for five is alive," he added.

When Cynthia stepped onto the ice to prepare for her skate, the crowd had yet to settle down. They hooted and hollered over Joannie's commanding performance. Cynthia carefully dodged a slew of stuffed animals that excited fans had thrown on the ice for Joannie! Although they were longtime competitors on the ice, the two skaters were also good friends. Cynthia could not help but smile for Joannie.

Back in the kiss and cry, Joannie and Manon embraced as her high marks were posted. Even with Cynthia still left to skate, Joannie had slammed the door shut on her competition. In the end she defeated her opposition by more than 33 points and won her fifth Canadian title!

Following the competition reporters crowded around Joannie. Not since Liz Manley won the silver medal at the 1988 World Championships had a Canadian woman landed on the medal podium. Could Joannie end the 21-year drought?

Next stop, the 2009 World Championships in Los Angeles, California!

2
Little Skater, Big Dreams

One cold day in Montreal, Quebec, on January 13, 1986, Normand and Therese Rochette welcomed a baby girl into their lives. The proud parents vowed to always protect and support their child in any path she chose.

They named their daughter Joannie Anne Rochette. As they looked at little Joannie bundled in a pink blanket, they never dreamed she would become one of Canada's all-time greatest female figure skaters.

Normand worked as a hockey coach in Berthierville, Quebec, a small, picturesque town 60 miles outside of Montreal. All day long Normand taught hockey to eager students. He often wondered if his little girl would someday love skating as much as he did. Sometimes Normand would lovingly cuddle Joannie in his arms and take her for a lap around the rink, so she could feel the incredible sensation of gliding on ice.

The Rochettes lived close to Berthierville in Ile Dupas, a tiny island in the middle of the St. Lawrence River with a population of only about 500 people. The family loved the serene town with its close-knit community.

When Joannie turned four years old, Normand decided it was time for her to try skating on her own. He carefully laced skates on her tiny feet. She wore beginner double runner blades that gave added stability so she could balance herself more easily as she got accustomed to standing on the slippery ice surface. Joannie immediately loved the sensation of floating on frozen water.

"I couldn't skate. I was just walking fast," Joannie recalled to the *Ottawa Sun*.

"Watch me! Watch me!" Joannie called to her parents as she giggled excitedly.

From that day forward Joannie wanted to skate all the time. Her parents even bought her skates with real razor-thin blades.

Joannie quickly became quite independent at the rink. She learned to glide along the ice and use her toe pick to stop. She discovered how to skate on one foot and do backward swizzles. She enjoyed how her soft blonde hair flew everywhere as she gathered speed during a lap.

Joannie's mother soon realized that her daughter took figure skating more seriously than most kids her age. She noticed that when Joannie skated for fun, even with a group of friends, she seemed very competitive.

Her parents enrolled their daughter in private lessons with coach Nathalie Riquier. Joannie soaked up her lessons. She learned how to do spirals, spins and even waltz jumps.

Joannie was an eager learner in the classroom as well. One day in elementary school, Joannie's teacher announced that the Olympic Games were approaching.

Joannie listened intently as her teacher told the class about Pierre de Coubertin, a man who believed that athletics were good for the body, mind and soul. In the late 1800s he revived the Olympic Games, a series of sporting events which determined the world's best athletes in various sports.

Joannie's teacher explained that de Coubertin once made a very beautiful comment about the Olympics. He said, "The important thing is not to win, but to take part." His quote became known as the best example of the Olympic spirit. Even if you finish last, it doesn't matter. It's enough to be part of such an honorable event.

A few weeks later the 1994 Lillehammer Olympics aired on television. Joannie sat transfixed by the beautiful ladies skaters who jumped and spun with such ease and grace. When her bedtime arrived Joannie asked her parents if she could finish watching the competition. They looked at their daughter's pleading blue eyes and softened. She could stay up past her bedtime for this special occasion.

Joannie's heart raced as American Nancy Kerrigan took the ice barely weeks after being brutally attacked by a member of a competitor's camp. Nancy skated wonderfully and the crowd stood in appreciation of her brave skate.

Then Oksana Baiul followed. Earlier that morning during a practice session, the Ukrainian orphan collided with Germany's

Tanja Szewczenko and badly bruised her lower back and shoulder. Would she be able to compete?

The dramatic skater circled the ice as she summoned the courage to skate her program. Finally, she assumed her starting pose.

Broadway show tunes played as Oksana flirted, jumped, and spun her way into the world's hearts. She didn't land as many clean triple jumps as Nancy, but the ballerina-like skater had an unmatched musical ability. When she finished her captivating performance, she clasped her hands to her head and burst into tears.

When her marks popped up on the scoreboard, Oksana and Nancy had tied, but in figure skating the skater with the highest artistic scores wins the tie breaker.

"Nancy's second. You're first," Oksana's coach, Galina Zmieyeva, shouted excitedly as Oksana wept all over again.

Even years later Joannie could not shake the memory of Oksana's dramatic Olympic victory.

"I still remember Oksana Baiul winning," Joannie told *International Figure Skating Magazine.* "It was so emotional for her. She was crying tears of joy, all that drama. I loved it. Whenever I think of the Olympics, I think of that."

That image inspired Joannie. She would pursue her figure skating dream, just like Oksana. She wanted to create her own Olympic magic.

3
Manon Perron

For the next four years, Joannie raced home from school, grabbed her figure skates and begged her mother to take her skating. She wanted to squeeze as much skating into the day as possible.

Joannie loved all parts of skating – spins, spirals, even cross-overs. Yet she enjoyed jumps most of all. She loved jumping into the air, spinning around and landing on the tiny sliver of the blade. Soon Joannie mastered all her double jumps: the Lutz, the flip, the loop, the Salchow, and the toe loop.

Joannie was also a good spinner. She could do a layback, a sit spin and a camel spin. Good spins required hours of practice, but the hard-working skater always rose to the challenge.

In 1998 Joannie spent much of February glued to her television set watching the Nagano Winter Olympics. In the ladies event she cheered for American Tara Lipinski. Joannie looked up to Tara and emulated her difficult jumping skills.

As Joannie watched, Tara and her teammate, Michelle Kwan, along with China's Lu Chen, skated the greatest Olympic ladies free skating competition to date. Tara became the youngest Olympic champion in history, while Michelle won the silver medal. Meanwhile, Lu won the bronze medal for a second straight Olympics.

The following year Joannie qualified for the 1999 Canadian Championships. The best Canadian skaters at different levels competed to determine the country's best skaters. Joannie skated at the novice level. When her plane landed in Ottawa, Ontario, she felt butterflies in her stomach. How would she compare against the other girls?

Now that Joannie competed at a high level, she skated two programs in every competition: a short program and a long program. The short program, sometimes called the technical program, required a combination jump, a solo jump and an Axel jump. It also called for spins, spirals and step sequences, known as footwork. The judges then ranked the skaters in order of how they performed all of the elements.

The long program, often dubbed the free skate, ran twice as long. Judges rated skaters on how well they executed jumps, spins, spirals and other elements. The judges ranked each skater in the long program. The short and long program placements were then added up. The skater with the lowest total won, the person with the second lowest total placed second, and so on.

Joannie struggled at her first Canadian championships. She placed 15th out of 16 competitors.

"I had a terrible skate," she later recalled to the *Ottawa Sun*. "It was a good experience, though, to see all the other skaters. After that year, I grew up a lot."

When Joannie returned home she decided to look for a new coach. The Rochettes chose esteemed coach Manon Perron, a skating veteran who coached a variety of skating disciplines, including ladies, men and pairs. She had a reputation for teaching sound technique and treating her students very well on and off the ice.

Manon had already seen Joannie at several ice skating seminars and thought she had natural jumping talent and strong skating skills. The experienced coach also noticed that Joannie had no idea how much natural talent she possessed.

Shortly after she began training with Manon, Joannie landed her first triple, the Salchow! After a year she learned four different triple jumps in all. Soon Joannie's stroking became more powerful. Her spins gained speed and improved positions. Her jumps grew bigger. Her overall consistency improved by leaps and bounds.

Skate Canada, her country's skating federation, took notice of Joannie's rapid improvement. They rewarded her hard work by sending her to an international competition in the Netherlands. Joannie loved meeting athletes from different backgrounds. Although the competitors spoke different languages, they shared one common bond: they loved figure skating!

In January 2000 Joannie returned to the Canadian championships on the novice level. The competition took place in Calgary, Alberta, host of the 1988 Winter Olympics.

Joannie felt great confidence heading into the competition. She now owned triple jumps and the rest of her skating had improved, too.

Joannie drew to skate second out of 12 skaters in the short program. She skated to her starting position and waited for her Spanish music to play. Joannie landed a good triple toe loop-double toe loop jump combination and a double Lutz for her solo jump. When she attempted her double Axel, though, she fell down hard. A determined Joannie sold the rest of her program. She would not let one mistake ruin her performance.

Joannie skated off the ice in disappointment. Yet Manon praised her student for not giving up after the mistake. She felt Joannie's performance still went well. When the short program competition concluded, the judges agreed with Manon. They placed Joannie second.

Joannie now had a great chance to win the Canadian novice title. If she won the long program, she would win the gold medal. Manon, however, cautioned the young skater to only focus on skating well. She did not want Joannie to think about placements.

The day of the long program, Joannie remembered her coach's advice. When the announcer called her name, she hit her start position, let out one final breath and performed her program to the best of her ability. In the end Joannie won the gold medal!

Joannie later stood proudly on the top step of the podium. She smiled as an official placed a gold medal around her neck. Joannie was now the Canadian ladies novice champion!

4
The Price of a Dream

Winning the novice title brought Joannie her first taste of television exposure. The TV channel CTV showed her winning program. People all across Canada watched her skate!

When Joannie arrived home she learned that Skate Canada had given her another international assignment. They would send her to the Mladost Trophy in Zagreb, Croatia. She could not wait to travel abroad again!

Joannie's competitors included skaters from Slovenia, Finland, Croatia and Japan. Among a field of nine skaters, Joannie won the silver medal. Japan's Miki Ando, who would someday become world champion, took home the gold medal.

Despite Joannie's success her family still had many skating bills to juggle. Next to equestrian, figure skating ranked as the most expensive sport to pursue in Canada. The expenses added up over time!

A skater pays for ice time, coaching lessons, choreography and various dance classes. Travel costs to competitions alone can total thousands of dollars!

Equipment can be costly as well. Elite skaters require custom skates which may cost around a thousand dollars. They also must budget their money for a minimum of two competition costumes a year, which can range from a few hundred dollars to a few thousand dollars!

Joannie's mother once told the newspaper *La Presse,* "I think that I would be discouraged if I started to calculate all the costs!"

Normand and Therese always budgeted their money carefully so they could cover their daughter's skating costs. They wanted to help Joannie pursue her big dream.

Joannie's parents supported her in other ways as well. Her father loved sharing advice and traveling to competitions to watch his daughter compete. His heart filled with pride when he watched his little girl skate. Meanwhile, Joannie's mother always made sure that her daughter remained well-rounded and treated school as seriously as skating.

"When I was a kid, my mother would watch me skate every day," Joannie remarked to *CBC Sports.* "She would sit through every lesson and make me do my homework while the ice was being flooded."

Joannie's support system also extended to her coach. She and Manon formed a close bond. Over time she began to think of Manon as a second mother.

Following her impressive novice success, Joannie continued her steady training and set her sights on winning the Canadian championships on the junior level.

At the start of the season, she flew to Lake Placid, New York, to compete in the 2000 North American Challenge Skate. Joannie finished first at the competition, becoming the first Canadian woman to ever win the event! A month later she collected another gold medal at the Minto Skate.

That fall Joannie competed on the Junior Grand Prix circuit. The International Skating Union (also known as the ISU) created the Grand Prix, a series of competitions hosted by a variety of countries over the course of several weeks. At the end of the series, the top six skaters competed in one last event for the honor of being crowned Grand Prix Final champion.

For Joannie's first assignment of the season, she competed in St. Gervais, France, and finished in fifth place. She then flew to Mexico City for Cup of Mexico and placed fourth in a tough field.

When December 2000 arrived Joannie and her family celebrated the holidays at home in Ile Dupas. On Christmas Eve the Rochettes ate a holiday feast. Joannie loved dessert time and always allowed herself a Christmas treat. After a delicious holiday dinner, the family sat around their beautifully decorated Christmas tree and opened presents from one another. Then they drove to church for a special holiday service.

Soon the 2001 Canadian Junior Championships arrived. Joannie, her family and Manon flew to Winnipeg, Manitoba. As the reigning novice champion, experts named Joannie as a favorite to win the junior ladies title, but the competition would not be a walk in the park. Courtney Sokal and Marie-Luc Jodoin, who stood on the podium with Joannie at the 2000 Canadian Novice Championships, could also win.

Joannie skated a solid short program to the mesmerizing "Rhapsody on a Theme of Paganini" to place first. She landed a triple loop-double toe loop combination, a nice triple flip out of footwork and a springy double Axel. The judges rewarded Joannie with the short program win.

Joannie arrived at the arena hours before her scheduled long program start time. She kept busy backstage by listening to music on her headphones and stretching to keep her muscles limber. Finally, Manon summoned her to the ice.

Joannie's performance to "Istanbul" and "Putting on the Ritz" in the long program started out strongly, but halfway through, she lost her concentration, awkwardly singling her triple loop. Joannie's body slumped in disappointment. She skated around the rink with little regard to her music and then stumbled awkwardly out of a triple Salchow. Then on her final jump, a triple flip, she stepped out of its landing, too. When her music finally finished, she dropped her head in dismay. Joannie was angry with herself for giving up on the presentation side of her program after she made the technical errors. She never wanted to make that mistake again.

Joannie felt sure the gold medal had slipped from her fingers, but she did not know that the other girls had also struggled. When the competition ended she had won the event!

With her back to back wins at the Canadian championships, reporters lined up to interview the young skater.

"Are you moving up to the senior level next year?" asked one reporter.

Joannie nodded. "I'd like to be in the top five next year," she said.

"No Canadian woman has ever won all three ladies figure skating titles – novice, junior and senior," said another reporter. "Do you think you can accomplish that?"

"We'll take it step by step," Manon answered protectively. "We want her to have fun while she improves."

With her competition over Joannie watched Jennifer Robinson win her fourth senior Canadian championship. Fifteen-year-old Nicole Watt placed second and Annie Bellemare took the bronze. Joannie could not believe that next year she would compete against them.

Thanks to her big win at the Canadian championships, Skate Canada named Joannie to the 2001 World Junior Championships in Sofia, Bulgaria. She placed eighth, delivering the highest placement by a Canadian woman in nearly ten years!

When Joannie arrived home she watched the 2001 World Championships on television. Her favorite, Irina Slutskaya, a spitfire Russian with powerful jumps, won her third world silver medal. She loved watching Irina soar on her gigantic jumps and bend her body into many unique positions during her blurring spins.

Joannie returned to the ice in late spring to prepare for her last year on the Junior Grand Prix. At her first event in Poland, she finished in fifth place.

A month later Joannie flew to Milan, Italy, for the final Junior Grand Prix event of her career. Joannie had fun touring the world's premiere fashion capital, but she was also hungry to place in the top three of the competition.

In the short program portion, Joannie finished fourth. Determined to add a Junior Grand Prix medal to her growing hardware collection, she fought hard for every jump in her long program. In the end she placed third overall!

As Joannie held her precious bronze medal, she felt satisfied with her journey as a junior skater.

Next stop, the senior ranks!

5
The New Kid in Town

Now a senior level skater, Joannie would compete at the Canadian championships against skaters with impressive resumes. How would she fare against them?

Manon told Joannie that in order to be taken seriously as a senior skater, she needed to strengthen her musical presentation. Joannie sometimes concentrated so hard on landing her jumps that she forgot about her music!

Manon suggested that Joannie become a character in her programs so she would become more involved in her performance. They created background stories for her short and long program characters. Joannie also worked to achieve better positions in her spins and spirals.

When Joannie arrived at the 2002 Canadian Championships in Hamilton, Ontario, television and print media roamed everywhere. More reporters than usual wandered backstage. Photographers packed the practice sessions.

The championships also doubled as the Olympic trials. Since Canada had only qualified one ladies berth for the Olympics, the competition for the lone spot looked fierce.

Most figured the winner would come from two candidates: Jennifer Robinson or Annie Bellemare. In the battle for the bronze, 2001 silver medalist Nicole Watt, 2000 Canadian junior champion Marianne Dubuc and Joannie were all contenders.

"I hope (Joannie can win a medal)," Manon told the *Ottawa Sun*. "But it's not the goal for her. It's to make the step up to senior."

Joannie agreed with her coach's outlook.

"The only thing that matters to me is my performance," Joannie confirmed to *SLAM! Sports*.

Shortly before the Canadian championships, the Rochette family experienced a serious scare. As Therese drove to the competition, another car hit her car. Joannie's mother survived the crash, but she was under considerable pain. She would experience recurring back problems for the rest of her life.

Joannie considered withdrawing from the competition, but her mom encouraged her to compete. Eventually, Joannie agreed to honor her wishes. She felt determined to skate well for her mother.

In the short program a nervous Joannie fell on her triple Lutz and sat in fifth place. On the other hand, Jennifer and Annie skated cleanly. The judges put Annie into first place, while a disappointed Jennifer settled for second.

Joannie fell on the Lutz in the long program, but she did not let mistakes affect her performances anymore. She rebounded from her error by landing four clean triple jumps in a pretty performance to "La Fete de Fleurs." She won the bronze medal!

Meanwhile, Jennifer skated a strong long program to earn a trip to the Salt Lake City Olympics. A crushed Annie fell to second place and watched her Olympic dreams disappear.

Joannie could not believe it when she sat beside Jennifer and Annie at the post-competition press conference. They were her heroes for so long. Now she sat right next to them! Joannie quickly learned that her idols were as nice in person as they always appeared on television.

When one reporter called Joannie the future of Canadian ladies figure skating, Jennifer smiled encouragingly at her. Then when Joannie experienced difficulty answering a question in English, Annie quickly helped her with the translation. Joannie felt grateful for Jennifer and Annie's kind gestures. She vowed that she would always emulate their good sportsmanship.

Following the ladies event Joannie traveled to Korea for the Four Continents Championships, an annual competition for skaters who represent the continents of the Americas, Asia, Africa and Australia. The competition allowed her the opportunity to compete against top international senior skaters. Joannie ended the competition in ninth place.

The following month Joannie competed at the 2002 World Junior Championships in Hamar, Norway. She beat her previous year's placement by finishing fifth.

Joannie reflected on her first senior season. She had won medals, met idols and visited different parts of the world. Joannie couldn't wait to see where skating would lead her next!

6
Away from Home

Jennifer Robinson's ninth place finish at the 2002 World Championships earned two Canadian ladies spots at the 2003 World Championships. Joannie only needed to move up one step on the Canadian podium to make her first world team.

One summer day when Joannie arrived at the rink for a training session, Manon asked to speak with her. She had life-changing news. Her husband's work was transferring him to Montreal and she would move with him. Joannie had to either find a new coach or move to Montreal to continue training with Manon.

Joannie and her parents explored her options. If Joannie moved to Montreal she would live away from her family. She would be so homesick! On the other hand, if she didn't follow Manon, she would need a new coach. Joannie couldn't imagine anyone else coaching her.

Then Joannie remembered her dream of skating in the Olympics someday. To achieve that lofty goal, skating must come first.

Joannie asked her parents if she could move to Montreal and continue training with Manon. Normand and Therese felt proud that their daughter wanted to make such a huge commitment. They would miss Joannie terribly, but they supported her wish and vowed to visit her often.

The Rochettes found a nice couple near Montreal who rented Joannie a room in their house. Joannie stayed with them during the week. On weekends she went home.

Joannie missed her parents and friends very much, but her skating always perked her up. She soon made friends with several skaters at her new rink.

Joannie also began training a triple-triple jump combination for the upcoming season. Then one day during practice, a sharp pain shot through her leg. It intensified whenever she jumped.

Joannie's doctor diagnosed her with shin splints, a muscle pain often caused by repetitive use. He advised her to stop the strenuous training, including jumping, for several weeks. Joannie felt devastated. Still, if she didn't follow her doctor's advice, her condition could worsen.

Reluctantly, Joannie and Manon made the difficult decision to withdraw from her fall assignments. Now the Canadian championships would mark Joannie's first competition of the season! Would she be ready in time?

A few weeks before the 2003 Canadian Championships, Joannie's doctor cleared her to resume training. In her first week back on the ice, a frustrated Joannie struggled to land even the simplest jumps. She thought about withdrawing from the competition but made the trip to Saskatchewan instead. A fighter, she would battle through the difficult struggle.

Jennifer Robinson seemed a shoo-in for a spot on the world team. Annie Bellemare and Joannie would likely battle for the final berth.

During her short program warm-up, Joannie felt more nervous than usual because she had not competed in nearly a year. As she circled the ice, Joannie gave herself a silent pep talk.

Finally, the comforting opening notes of her program's music began. She made one minor jump error, but she concluded with a strong spiral sequence and a fast, centered spin. Joannie's effort put her in third place.

One spot separated Joannie from a trip to the world championships. A goal she dreamed about for years was within her grasp. Could she reach it with so little training time behind her?

On the day of the long program, Joannie stood by the boards before her free skate and soaked up her coach's last minute advice. She took a deep breath and skated out to her start position with steely determination. Could Joannie win a spot on the world team, especially while recovering from an injury?

Joannie fought for every jump in her program. When the competition ended she couldn't believe her final placement. She won the silver medal and a trip to the world championships!

Meanwhile, Jennifer became the first woman in 71 years to win six Canadian titles. The classy competitor celebrated her achievement, but she also lavished praise on Joannie.

"For her to come here after not training as much as she'd liked because of the shin splints she had, that's awesome," Jennifer said.

"She's capable of doing a lot of great things for this sport," she continued. "It's cool we're going (to worlds) together."

The following month Joannie flew to Beijing, China, for the Four Continents Championships. A formidable Japanese team of Fumie Suguri, Shizuka Arakawa and Yukari Nakano swept the podium. Joannie finished eighth. More notably, she beat Jennifer in the short program.

Once back home Joannie began training for the world championships. She soon learned sad news. Irina Slutskaya had withdrawn from the world championships citing concern for her mother's health. Her hero would remain home with her mom, who remained on dialysis as she awaited a kidney transplant.

In late March Joannie traveled to Washington, D.C., for the 2003 World Championships. A few months earlier she thought her season might end prematurely. Now Joannie would skate against the world's best! From the moment she landed in America, Joannie felt overwhelmed by the competition's top skaters.

On a cool Wednesday morning, Joannie arrived at the MCI Center to skate in her qualifying round. She walked into the ladies locker room and found herself looking straight at Michelle Kwan! Joannie felt so star struck she could barely whisper, "hello," when her idol warmly greeted her.

Joannie nervously placed her athletic bag on a bench. When she looked up again, Olympic champion Sarah Hughes had entered the room! Joannie wanted to strike up a conversation with her but she felt too shy.

Later as her group warmed up, Joannie could not concentrate on her skating. Instead she stared at Sarah and Michelle.

"I couldn't help but watch them in warm-up," Joannie told *SLAM! Sports*. "I just wanted to sit down and watch them."

When it came time to skate, Joannie had not warmed up well enough. She landed only three clean triples in her program and finished a disappointing 18th.

Joannie quickly learned a valuable lesson from that mistake. For the short program warm-up, she concentrated only on herself. As a result she skated a solid short program with a triple flip-double toe loop combination, a slightly two-footed triple Lutz and a great double Axel.

Although Joannie's long program did not go so smoothly, she enjoyed watching the other skaters compete for medals. She cheered for Michelle Kwan as she won her fifth world title before a home crowd. Russian Elena Sokolova nabbed the silver medal in a stunning jumping display, and Japan's Fumie Suguri won her second straight world bronze medal. Joannie admired how all the top women remained calm under such intense pressure.

They look so comfortable and confident on the ice, Joannie thought. *I have a lot to learn from them. I would like to be that way, too*.

Already Joannie thought of how she would apply lessons learned toward future competitions. Already she looked forward to next season.

7
Expectations

Joannie accomplished a lot last season while overcoming a serious injury. Imagine what she could achieve if she remained healthy!

Early that summer Joannie received invitations to Skate Canada and Cup of Russia. She looked forward to competing on the Senior Grand Prix in the fall.

At the same time figure skating underwent a huge transformation as the sport extinguished the 6.0 scoring system and ushered in a new judging system called Code of Points (COP). The system judged skaters on the strength of their jumps, spins, spirals and step sequences using a base value of points and grade of execution. Judges also rated the artistic merit of a routine, or the program components. The skater with the highest overall point total won.

Manon and Joannie welcomed the challenge of the new judging system. They worked to maximize as many points as possible for her programs.

When practices for Skate Canada began, Joannie skated so well that people began buzzing about her! Some even predicted she would win a medal. Instead of enjoying the attention, Joannie grew self-conscious and jittery. She suddenly felt overwhelming pressure to live up to such big predictions.

By the time the competition began, Joannie's nervousness showed. She finished a disastrous 10th. A few weeks later the spunky skater rebounded nicely to finish fourth at Cup of Russia, missing the bronze medal by a mere .54 points.

Later that winter Joannie received an invitation to participate in the Celebration on Ice tour. Brian Orser, Kurt Browning and Elvis Stojko headlined the tour. World champion ice dancers Shae-Lynn Bourne and Victor Kraatz also used the opportunity to stage their farewell performance. Joannie felt intimidated but also thrilled to share the ice with the cast of skating legends.

Joannie entered the 2004 Canadian Championships in Edmonton as a medal favorite. Some predicted she might even end Jennifer Robinson's lengthy reign as Canadian champion.

The buzz for Joannie intensified after she won her qualifying group by landing six triples and earning a standing ovation. Jennifer won the other qualifying group, but she struggled with her jumps. Her marks were also not as high as Joannie's.

Unfortunately, Joannie made two serious jumping mistakes in the short program two days later. She slipped to a devastating fifth.

Fifteen-year-old Cynthia Phaneuf provided the night's biggest surprise. A lyrical skater with big jumps, she electrified the crowd to win the short program. A poor qualifying round kept her from taking first place overall.

Later that night Joannie lay in bed tossing and turning. She replayed her short program in her mind. She had made a silly mistake on a double axel, a jump she had learned when she was ten years old! She desperately wanted a do-over.

The next morning Joannie waited behind the boards as Cynthia finished her long program to thunderous applause. Joannie's nerves intensified. She tried to block out the roaring crowd as Manon urged her to fight hard for every element in her program.

When her music began Joannie launched into a mesmerizing array of sparkling jumps, spins, spirals and footwork. The audience rose a second straight time. Flowers rained from the sky.

Moments later, Joannie beamed in the kiss and cry as she celebrated her strong performance. She felt proud for rebounding after a difficult short program.

Although Joannie beat Cynthia in the long program, she could not pass her in the overall standings. She sat in second place.

When Jennifer took the ice, the Canadian champion looked visibly nervous. She ended up skating her weakest long program in years. The veteran dropped to third overall. Cynthia became the unexpected Canadian champion and Joannie repeated as silver medalist.

Joannie could not believe she had won the silver medal again. It marked the first time Joannie beat Jennifer in competition. Her second place finish also meant that she would return to the world championships!

Then in a controversial decision, Skate Canada only named Cynthia to the junior world team and assigned Joannie and Jennifer to the senior world championships. The new Canadian champion would attend senior worlds only as a spectator.

A couple of weeks later, Joannie finished fourth at the Four Continents Championships in Hamilton, Ontario. Cynthia won the silver medal, while Japan's Yukina Ota took the title.

The media suddenly pushed Joannie aside. They quickly set their sights on promoting Cynthia as the next great Canadian skating star. Joannie could not help but notice that some people now viewed her as an afterthought.

Although she had recorded her best finish ever at Four Continents, a disappointed Joannie did not celebrate her fourth place. She had raised her standards for her results.

"Maybe a year ago it was good for me but it's not good enough anymore," she told *TSN*.

Joannie shelved her disappointment to participate in the skating gala. She donned a black, sparkly one-piece outfit to skate to Vanessa Carlton's version of "Paint It Black." Joannie smiled throughout her performance. She loved performing to music she listened to in her spare time.

After Four Continents concluded Joannie joined the *Celebration on Ice* tour and trained for worlds in her spare time. Many experienced cast members watched Joannie's practice sessions with interest. They even offered tips on her jumps and other elements. Joannie soaked up their valuable advice. She felt fortunate to receive help from her respected peers.

By the time the 2004 World Championships arrived in late March, Joannie felt a surge of confidence in her skating. When she and Manon boarded a plane headed to Dortmund, Germany, she felt determined to prove that she deserved to compete with the world's best skaters. She refused to be anyone's afterthought.

From the moment she stepped onto the practice ice, Joannie commanded everyone's attention with her consistent jumps. During one practice she even landed the quadruple toe loop, a jump few female skaters ever attempted! Her unparalleled jumping display drew gasps from the knowledgeable crowd.

The short program began on a Friday. Joannie skated well in the short program, landing every jump perfectly. She also displayed crisp spins and an energetic footwork display. The judges placed her ninth. Although many thought she deserved a higher placement, Joannie felt pleased with her result.

A few seconds into her long program, Joannie fell on her first jump, the triple loop. She refused to let that mistake disrupt her program, though. She rebounded quickly to land the triple Lutz, a big triple flip, a triple toe, another triple flip, a second triple toe and a triple Salchow. As the crowd erupted with enthusiasm, she landed a double Axel. She had never given up.

Later in the kiss and cry, Manon patted her student happily on the knee. When Joannie's presentation marks came up, the skater's eyes lit up. She felt ecstatic when she finished in eighth place. When she arrived in Germany, Joannie never dreamed she would place in the top ten. Now she was top eight in the world!

Following a 14th place finish, a cheerful Jennifer Robinson addressed the press backstage. "I am officially retired," she said. "I am announcing it right now."

Joannie wished Jennifer all the best as she embarked on a professional career. She felt honored to have had such a great role model for a teammate.

After worlds concluded the prestigious *Champions on Ice* tour asked Joannie to join their company as a guest skater. She would skate in the New York show with legends like Irina Slutskaya, Michelle Kwan and Evgeny Plushenko. Joannie's career had reached a new plateau!

8
The Breakup

Now a top ten skater in the world, Joannie spent the summer in high demand. She accepted several invitations to perform in various ice shows. In addition she conducted many seminars all across Canada. She also joined the farewell tour of two-time Olympic pairs bronze medalists Isabelle Brasseur and Lloyd Eisler. If her life wasn't busy enough, she also devoted seven days a week toward her college classes!

Not everyone felt thrilled with Joannie's jammed schedule. Manon frowned at her student's many commitments. She believed that Joannie's skating had begun to suffer from lack of practice.

Manon's frustration grew when Joannie sometimes arrived late to practices. She argued that her pupil's chaotic schedule had negatively impacted her training. Joannie had lost consistency with her jumps and looked generally unmotivated. Their disagreements often interrupted their training sessions. Manon complained that her pupil did not take her practice seriously, while Joannie argued that her coach treated her like a child.

Their differences finally reached a boiling point right before the new season began. One weekend Joannie entered a small competition in Montreal. She skated a disastrous long program landing only one triple jump. It was the worst she had ever skated.

Later that week Manon called Joannie with shocking news. She was ending their partnership. Manon would no longer tolerate her student's half-hearted efforts.

Joannie burst into tears. Her relationship with Manon had felt strained lately, but she did not want a new coach. She could not imagine training with anyone else.

With the new season quickly approaching, the Rochettes discussed Joannie's training options. They eventually decided on the coaching team of Josee Normand and former Canadian champion Sebastien Britten in Brossard, Quebec.

When Joannie arrived at the Ecole les 4 Glaces rink several days later, she carried a heavy heart and a bruised ego. Joannie spent nearly all of her first day with her new coaches in tears. To worsen matters, she looked sluggish and poorly trained.

Each day eventually got progressively better. Though Joannie still missed Manon, she adjusted to her new rink. In fact, her former coach's dismissal of her lit a fire under Joannie. She threw herself into her training. Her body slowly returned to competitive shape.

At her first competition under new coaches, Cup of China, Joannie fell on her combination jump in the short program. The judges still seemed impressed with the other strong elements in her "Dumky Piano Trio" program and placed her fourth.

In her "Firebird" long program, Joannie showed several impressive jumping passes. She landed five triples to finish third. As Joannie accepted her bronze medal, she smiled shyly at Irina Slutskaya who stood atop the podium. She felt thrilled to share the medal stand with her.

Joannie next jetted to Paris, France, for her second Grand Prix competition. She skated perfectly to win the short program. The next day Joannie landed six clean triples in the long program to win the competition over second place finisher, Italy's Carolina Kostner. Joannie's win qualified her for the Grand Prix Final!

In mid-December Joannie and her coaches returned to Beijing, China, for the Grand Prix Final. She skated a strong short program and moved into third place.

The morning of the long program, Joannie awoke with butterflies in her stomach. She hoped to leave China with another medal, but she felt so nervous! Joannie then reminded herself how much she loved her "Firebird" program. She would enjoy that day's performance.

A few hours later Joannie did just that. She landed four triples to win the bronze medal. Irina won gold and Shizuka Arakawa finished second.

When Joannie arrived in London, Ontario, for the 2005 Canadian Championships, she vowed to enjoy herself the entire week. If she had fun, her skating would fall into place.

Throughout the week Joannie gave interviews to various news outlets. Most asked how she handled her break-up with Manon.

"I think she did it for me," Joannie remarked to the *Ottawa Sun*. "She wanted the best for me."

"It was very, very hard for me," she continued. "I had been with Manon since I was very young."

On the day of the short program, Joannie looked beautiful in her dark costume. She sped across the ice with carefree abandon and soaring jumps. Joannie easily won the short program, earning a prolonged standing ovation from the adoring crowd.

"It was the best I've skated under that much pressure," Joannie told the *London Free Press*.

Over 7,000 spectators gathered to watch the ladies long program, among them, Manon, who sat in the stands cheering on her former student. She still cared deeply for Joannie and wanted her to fulfill her enormous potential.

Joannie's program began with a perfect triple toe-triple toe combination. Then she landed a triple Lutz, a triple loop, a double Axel, a triple Lutz-double toe loop combination, a triple flip-triple toe combination, and another double Axel. She grinned widely when she landed her final jump. As she spun her last spin, Joannie couldn't even hear her music over the roar of the crowd!

Moments later Joannie's mouth dropped in astonishment at her high marks. She placed her hands to her face in disbelief. Joannie won the 2005 Canadian title with what many considered the greatest performance in Canadian ladies skating. She also became the first Canadian skater to win senior, junior and novice ladies crowns. Cynthia Phaneuf settled for the silver medal, while up-and-comer Mira Leung took third place.

"I skated this for myself," Joannie told the *Ottawa Sun.* "I can't explain how good I felt."

When reporters prodded Joannie for her reaction to her performance, she needed only one word.

"Magical," she beamed.

That night Joannie celebrated her big victory in a quiet evening with her parents and friends. She had no idea that she was quickly becoming a celebrity!

The following day Joannie walked by a row of newspaper stands and saw herself on the front page! When she later returned to her hotel for some rest, she shared an elevator ride with a group of guests who instantly recognized her!

When Joannie and her parents returned home, Berthierville showered the youngest Rochette with love, throwing a festival in her honor. Joannie felt overwhelming emotion as she rode in a limousine while well-wishers lined the street cheering for their hometown girl.

However, Joannie learned that with success comes high expectations. Soon everyone expected her to win a medal at the upcoming world championships.

Sadly, Joannie's medal chances suddenly looked grim when she suffered a muscle strain in training one day. She also experienced boot problems, and painful sores developed on the heels of her feet. Joannie and her coaches opted to keep her physical issues quiet. They did not want people to think they were making excuses if she did not skate well at worlds.

Joannie arrived at the 2005 World Championships in Moscow, Russia, with her physical ailments still plaguing her. She also carried an enormous amount of stress. Not surprisingly, she had a poor competition and finished 11th. Her dream of winning a world medal would have to wait another year.

Irina snagged an emotional victory with a stunning long program. Sasha Cohen placed second and Carolina Kostner won the bronze medal.

After the world championships Joannie reflected on her season. Her injury now healing, Joannie's Olympic dream was only a few months away. She should have been happy but she felt empty instead. Something seemed missing from her skating. *Someone* seemed missing.

Joannie imagined the upcoming season. For years she had always dreamed of competing at the Olympics with Manon in her corner. She wanted to skate onto the Olympic ice knowing that Manon stood supportively by her side.

Joannie needed to take control of her own future now. Without hesitating, she picked up the telephone…

9

Love Song

Manon felt pleasantly surprised by Joannie's call.

"I thought she would have made her mom (call me) for her," Manon told the *Ottawa Sun*. "When she did it herself, I thought 'She understands. She knows what she has to do.' I don't have to tell her what to do anymore."

When Manon and Joannie resumed their professional partnership, they reached a new understanding. If Joannie arrived late to practice, she would be forbidden from skating that session. In exchange Joannie asked that her coach treat her more like a grown-up.

At first Joannie and Manon struggled to find the comfort level that once came so easily to them. As the weeks passed, though, their awkwardness disappeared.

When choosing her short program, Joannie felt adamant about skating to a form of popular music. She knew that billions would watch the Olympics, and she wanted people all over the world to recognize and enjoy her music. One afternoon she came across an instrumental version of Madonna's "Like a Prayer." A huge Madonna fan, Joannie had found her short program music.

While selecting her long program music, Joannie narrowed it down to two haunting pieces, "Les Feuilles Mortes" and "Hymne a l'amour." Manon suggested they combine both pieces and Joannie eagerly agreed.

One day Joannie and her mother were driving in their family car en route to an errand. Excited, Joannie wanted to share her Olympic long program music with her mom. She popped the music CD into the car's player. When Therese heard the opening notes of the music, she began to weep softly. Joannie sat stunned by her mother's reaction.

Therese then shared a story from her past. As a young woman in her 20s, she fell in love with a man who asked her to marry him. Two weeks before their wedding, tragedy struck. Therese's fiancée died in an accident.

Therese fell into a deep depression. During those terribly sad times, she found comfort in the song, "Hymne a l'amour." The song's lyrics centered on a loved one's death. Over time she began to think of the musical piece as *her* song.

After a period of mourning, Therese resumed her day-to-day activities. Her heart still ached but her life had to continue.

One day Therese met a man named Normand Rochette and she discovered she could fall in love again. When he proposed to her, she happily accepted.

A few years later Therese and Normand welcomed a beautiful baby boy into their lives. They felt so blessed. Tragically, their little boy died shortly after his birth. Devastated, Therese and Normand grieved for their son. Again, Therese listened to "Hymne a l'amour" during her grieving process.

The death of a child might tear some families apart, but Therese and Normand only grew closer. Their love for one another only deepened.

Then one day Therese discovered she was expecting another baby. Nine months later Joannie entered the world.

Therese's story touched Joannie deeply. She had no idea what relevance the song played in her parents' lives when she picked the music. Suddenly, it felt like fate had led her to the music.

At that moment Joannie dedicated her long program to her parents. Whenever she would skate to the music, she would remember how her parents love had survived through so much heartache.

St. John's, Newfoundland, hosted that season's Skate Canada. When Joannie arrived to compete at the competition, many people were naturally curious about her reconciliation with her coach.

"I've realized I just like working with Manon," Joannie explained to the *Ottawa Sun*. "The question was, who did I want beside the boards, who did I want to go with me to competitions and share the moment of my life? I see her more than my own parents. So that's why I went back to Manon."

Joannie wore a lovely white lace dress with delicate spaghetti straps as she skated to "Like a Prayer" for the first time in competition. During her detailed footwork section, the crowd clapped along to the music with great enthusiasm. She finished the short program in third place.

The next day Joannie arrived at Mile One Stadium in her warm-up suit. She stretched as she prepared for her long program. Joannie always warmed-up before she skated. She had to get all of her muscles slowly moving so she didn't pull them later when she skated intensely.

Then Joannie headed to the ladies locker room. She exchanged smiles with several other competitors when she entered the room. Joannie then changed into a light pink spaghetti strap dress that showcased her beautifully toned arms.

Joannie completed six big triple jumps in the long program. She grinned broadly as she and Manon exchanged an excited hug after her performance. When the final results were posted, Joannie moved up a spot to collect the silver medal.

Joannie then flew to Paris, France, to compete at Trophee Eric Bompard. Though she unleashed seven triples in the long program, Joannie finished fourth in a steep field.

On January 1st Joannie rang in the New Year. A ripple of excitement ran through her as cheers of "Happy 2006!" echoed throughout the room. The Olympic year had finally arrived!

Joannie had to first qualify for the Olympics, though. She knew what she needed to do. If Joannie placed in the top two at the Canadian championships, she would earn a ticket to the Torino Olympics.

Shortly before Canadians Joannie felt very sad when Cynthia Phaneuf withdrew from the competition due to a knee injury. She knew her fellow competitor felt crushed to miss out on an Olympic opportunity.

With the Olympics on the horizon, media requests poured in for the Canadian champion. Reporters asked Joannie if she felt nervous about defending her Canadian title.

"I'm just trying not to think about it," Joannie told the *Ottawa Sun*. "I want to skate well, have fun and see all my friends again at nationals."

Joannie handily won the qualifying round and short program at the 2006 Canadian Championships.

On the day of the ladies long program, Joannie walked into the Ottawa Civic Centre with a bright smile. The day marked her 20th birthday and she intended to give herself the best present of her life: a trip to the Olympics!

Joannie landed six triple jumps in a beautiful performance. As she sat in the kiss and cry awaiting her marks, the crowd sang rousing renditions of "Happy Birthday" to her in English and French.

Joannie easily cruised to her second Canadian title. She was officially an Olympian!

Sixteen-year-old Mira Leung finished with the silver medal, also making the Olympic and world team. Lesley Hawker placed third with a strong long program.

"This was definitely the best birthday I could wish for," Joannie told the *Ottawa Citizen*.

10
2006 Olympics: Torino

In the weeks before the Olympics, Joannie experienced the biggest media blitz of her career. Everyone wanted to interview her! Joannie tried to accommodate the various news outlets, but she and Manon also took care to ensure that she stayed focused on her skating. She wanted to skate her very best at the Olympics. Joannie also set a goal to place in the top ten in Torino.

"I want to live the whole experience," Joannie told the *Edmonton Sun*. "This is once in a lifetime and you don't want to miss any of it."

When Joannie arrived in Italy, she marveled at the stunning snow-capped Alps overlooking the picturesque city. It seemed like a wonderful dream.

The next day Joannie met Manon for her first Olympic practice. She looked in awe at the famous Olympic rings in the middle of the rink. Pierre de Coubertin designed the famous symbol to represent passion, faith, victory, work ethic and sportsmanship.

On February 10, 2006, Joannie marched in the Opening Ceremonies. She felt overwhelmed walking into Olympic Stadium behind Canadian flag bearer and hockey star Danielle Goyette. She got goose bumps when five Olympic rings rose from the ground and were illuminated with fireworks.

At the Olympic village Joannie met numerous athletes, including Clara Hughes, a Canadian cyclist and speed skater, who had won medals in both the summer and winter Olympics, and short track speed skater Francois-Louis Tremblay whom Joannie later watched win two silver medals.

When Joannie arrived at the Palavela Arena for the ladies short program, the atmosphere backstage felt incredibly tense.

"I thought I'd be so nervous my legs would shake so much I wouldn't be able to skate," she later told the *Edmonton Sun*.

When she reached center ice, Joannie soaked in the significance of the experience.

"You skate and there are the Olympic rings stamped onto the ice," she continued. "It means so much. The crowd is big but that's not what is the most meaningful. It's the rings."

Unfortunately, Joannie stumbled on her triple flip and finished ninth in the short program. Sasha Cohen grabbed a slight lead over Irina Slutskaya, while Shizuka Arakawa followed closely in third place.

Two days later Joannie waited to skate her long program. She knew that her parents sat in the stands ready to watch her compete on the world's biggest stage. She wanted to skate well for them.

As she listened carefully to Manon's final advice, Team Canada cheered heartily for Joannie. Several of her teammates waved Canadian flags to show their support. Seconds later she assumed her starting pose.

Joannie could not have skated her long program much better. She landed six fabulous triple jumps and drew big applause for her textbook spinning. When her program ended she raised her hands in triumph as the audience clapped, hollered and whistled with great enthusiasm. She closed her eyes as if she wanted to record the moment in her memory forever.

Joannie climbed to fifth place, nabbing the highest Olympic finish by a Canadian ladies skater since Liz Manley won silver in Calgary nearly twenty years earlier! She even recorded the second highest technical score of the entire ladies long program event.

Meanwhile, Shizuka became the first Japanese figure skater to win an Olympic gold medal. Sasha placed second and Irina finished third.

Thanks to Joannie's high finish, organizers of the exhibition gala invited her to perform in the esteemed show. She would skate on Olympic ice once more!

Dressed in a light blue costume that highlighted her beautiful eyes, Joannie skated to Madonna's vocal version of "Like a Prayer." The audience clapped to the music enthusiastically as the Canadian champion turned in a spirited performance.

"I had an amazing two weeks," Joannie said afterwards. "I'm going to remember this forever."

At the emotional Closing Ceremonies, Canadian opera sensation Ben Heppner sang "O Canada." In four years, athletes would gather in Vancouver, Canada, for the 2010 Olympic Games.

"I want to be in Vancouver," Joannie confided to *CTV*. "Hopefully I can win a medal there."

The countdown to the 2010 Olympic Games had officially begun!

11

Heartbreak

Joannie's emotional high came crashing down when she returned home. While she competed in Torino, her training mate, Andreanne Rousseau, lost her life in a car accident.

Joannie attended Andreanne's funeral to say goodbye to her friend. She grieved for her rink mate, vowing to cherish the good times they shared.

Joannie then resumed training for the 2006 World Championships in Calgary. When Shizuka Arakawa and Irina Slutskaya withdrew from the competition, Joannie became the third ranked skater at the world championships.

Joannie also learned that Ile Dupas had bestowed a huge honor on her. The proud town voted to name a street after her! Joannie felt so overwhelmed the first time she saw her name on the street sign.

The day before her daughter left for worlds, Therese lovingly washed Joannie's costumes by hand. Unfortunately, both dresses should have been dry cleaned only! The costumes shrunk so badly that they no longer fit. Joannie burst into tears. Costume designer

Josiane Lamond worked through the night fixing the dresses. Later as Joannie held her fixed costumes in her hands, she giggled over the drama that had unfolded. It felt good to laugh again.

From the moment Joannie's feet touched soil in Calgary, home of the 1988 Olympics, Canadians discussed her medal chances. Podium talk intensified after Joannie won her qualifying group.

At the post-qualifying round press conference, Joannie fielded questions about her performance. Suddenly, a reporter asked her how she had handled Andreanne's death. Joannie struggled to maintain her composure.

"It was very heartbreaking," Joannie told the *Ottawa Sun*. "I know (Andreanne) is with me now."

Joannie then excused herself. She only made it halfway down the hall before she doubled over in anguish. Manon held a sobbing Joannie in her arms while cameras followed in an attempt to film the private moment.

Perhaps still distracted two days later, Joannie made a costly jump error right off the bat in her short program. Flustered, she also singled her double Axel. The Canadian audience groaned in disappointment for her. When the short and qualifying programs were added up, Joannie hovered in fifth place overall.

Unlike some skaters who refused to meet the press after a disappointing performance, Joannie walked backstage and bravely faced reporters.

"Of course, I'm sad," she began. "I'm capable of much more. This week I've been skating very good in practice. I don't remember missing a jump since I arrived here."

"It was really hard to skate last because I knew everyone in the final warm-up at worlds is going to skate good," she continued. "I had that pressure, I prefer skating earlier, but that doesn't matter. You have to skate anyway. The mistake just happened because of a lack of focus."

Joannie didn't have much time to fret over her placement. Several hours later, she returned to the ice to practice for the next day's long program.

On a chilly Saturday afternoon, skating fans collected to witness the crowning of a new world champion. Sasha Cohen skated a shaky long program, but fellow American Kimmie Meissner followed with a tour de force performance containing two triple-triple combination jumps. The crowd roared with approval when she passed Sasha in the standings. Fumie Suguri also skated very well and squeaked past Sasha for second place.

Joannie had difficulty concentrating when her turn arrived. The circumstances of the last few weeks weighed her down. Her jumps fell apart. She lost her fight. When her music ended she stared off into space as if she were imagining the program she might have skated.

After she received her seventh place finish, Joannie sighed heavily and wiped tears from her eyes. When she had arrived in Calgary, she had believed she might finally win that elusive world medal. Now she had to wait another year - again.

"I'm very disappointed that it didn't happen for me," she said sadly backstage. "It was really tough skating after such a great performance. I didn't see it behind the curtain but I could hear the crowd."

"The battle was in my head, not my body," she added honestly.

Three weeks later Joannie embarked on the *Stars on Ice* tour as a full-time cast member for the first time. Although Joannie knew most of the skaters on the tour, she still felt timid around her heroes.

Soon though Joannie relaxed and became good friends with her cast mates. *Stars on Ice* boasted a tight knit company. Joannie spent a great deal of time with her buddy Jeffrey Buttle. 2002 Olympic pairs champion David Pelletier grew so fond of Joannie, he "adopted" her as his little sister.

The youngest company member, Joannie appreciated that the skaters looked after her with a strong protectiveness. She enjoyed the cast's group outings especially when they took a bike trip around Victoria.

Every night during the show, she performed a solo number to Celine Dion's "Vole." Joannie thought of Andreanne as she floated across the ice to the song lyrics about a young girl who lost her life too soon.

On the tour's final night, Joannie skated to the music one final time. Then she closed the door on the most emotional season of her life.

12
Changes

Big changes happened in Joannie's life during the off-season. For starters she began dating Francois-Louis Tremblay, the speed skater with whom she struck up a friendship at the Torino Games. Joannie enjoyed having a boyfriend, especially someone who understood the difficult life of a competitive athlete.

They say opposites attract, and the two sweethearts soon discovered they were indeed quite different. Joannie often struggled with nerves before a competition. Francois-Louis, on the other hand, rarely got nervous when he competed. His calming influence often helped Joannie collect her composure before a big competition.

One day Francois-Louis gave Joannie a stuffed monkey as a gift. She named it "Mr. Monkey." Whenever she traveled anywhere, "Mr. Monkey" went with her.

Joannie also decided to switch things up on the ice. Turning to renowned choreographer Sandra Bezic for her short program, Joannie found the courage to try a new style. They chose an instrumental version of Jimi Hendrix's blues song "Little Wing."

For her long program choreography, Joannie and David Wilson picked a Spanish piece, "Don Juan." Joannie even took flamenco lessons to prepare for the challenge.

Joannie had an uneven start to the season. She won Skate Canada but fell to fourth at her second assignment, Trophee Eric Bompard.

After the Grand Prix she resumed her studies and also trained for the Canadian championships. Life moved quickly for a competitive figure skater.

Halifax, Nova Scotia, won the bid to host the 2007 Canadian Championships. Although experts viewed Joannie as the overwhelming favorite to win the ladies title, several determined skaters nipped at her heels. Cynthia Phaneuf had returned to the ice and looked forward to competing again. The consistent Mira Leung also wanted a Canadian title.

"When you're winning for the first time, you're chasing the first prize," Joannie told the *Toronto Star*. "But when you're the winner one year, the next year the girls look at you, they watch you more."

In the end Joannie won her third Canadian title despite several jump errors. Mira repeated as silver medalist, Lesley Hawker finished third and Cynthia placed fourth in her comeback bid.

"I am happy I won," Joannie told reporters after the competition. "But I did not skate like I could."

The next month while battling the flu, Joannie flew to the Four Continents Championships in Colorado Springs, Colorado, where she won the short program.

During the next day's long program practice, Joannie accidentally collided with American Emily Hughes on the ice. Fortunately, neither skater suffered any injuries. They quickly apologized to one another before resuming their respective practices. Later in the locker room, they shared a laugh over their collision.

In the long program Joannie felt the strain of her illness. She missed several jumps and finished with the bronze medal. Kimmie Meissner took first place and Emily won the silver medal.

Throughout the entire 2007 season, Joannie never looked completely in her element. Perhaps she had experienced some plain old bad luck. Maybe she just felt let down after the thrill of the Olympics. Whatever the reason her skating seemed off all season long.

When Joannie traveled to Tokyo, Japan, for the 2007 World Championships, her medal prospects looked extremely dim.

During the prior year the ISU voted to eliminate the qualifying round at the world championships. The ladies competition began with the crucial short program.

Joannie struggled throughout her short program. She downgraded her combination jump and landed her Lutz off balance. To make matters worse she fell on her straight line footwork sequence. She ended the night in a humiliating 16th place.

Teammate Mira Leung fared even worse all the way back in 24th place.

Joannie's low placement alarmed many in the Canadian skating community. Canada suddenly looked in danger of losing a spot at the next year's worlds. Joannie's country needed their champion to snap out of a season-long funk.

When asked if she could rebound in the long program, Joannie answered confidently, "I know I can do it!"

So far Joannie's 2007 season had gone disappointingly. She refused to end the season on a down note.

Joannie's determination helped her place fifth in the free skate with an overall tenth place finish. Canada would keep two ladies spots for the 2008 World Championships. A true fighter, Joannie had skated her best effort at the most important competition of the season.

13

The Comeback

Joannie viewed the 2007-08 season as a comeback season. She vowed to restablish herself as one of the top skaters on the international scene.

Although she now lived on her own, Joannie cherished her close bond with her mother very much. After her disappointing results the previous season, she asked her mother to offer feedback on her training. So once a week Therese made the drive to Montreal to watch her daughter's training session and provide motherly advice.

Manon and Joannie also analyzed the mental aspects of her skating. A conscientious young woman, Joannie often over thought when she competed. If Joannie could perform without so many distractions cluttering her mind, she would skate with more freedom.

Joannie even began working with a sports psychologist. They discussed the fears and anxieties that negatively impacted her skating and found ways to overcome the problems. Joannie's confidence slowly returned.

Joannie kept her "Don Juan" long program for another year. For her short program she selected two piano concertos, one from Robert Schumann and another by Peter Tchaikovsky.

Joannie kicked off the Grand Prix season with third place finishes at Skate Canada and Cup of Russia.

Ever since her fifth place showing at the Olympics, Joannie also discovered that her popularity had grown.

"A lot of people didn't know me before [the Olympics] but they know me now," she admitted.

On one occasion Joannie went to a salon to have her hair styled. When she told the hairdresser that she was a figure skater, he asked if she knew Joannie Rochette. She giggled and politely informed him that she *was* Joannie Rochette!

Joannie worked hard at the rink everyday, but when she returned home, she allowed herself to relax. Sometimes Francois-Louis would cook dinner for her. He loved cooking so much that Joannie began to lovingly refer to him as her personal chef. She often helped her boyfriend cook so she could learn a few recipes herself. Although she wasn't a very good cook, she still enjoyed the learning process. Francois-Louis would often prepare an omelet or a delicious salad. The two would then discuss their respective days over a romantic dinner. Sometimes they even watched a movie afterwards. Joannie's favorite films included *The Shawshank Redemption* and *The Notebook*.

When the winter holidays arrived, Joannie celebrated them with her family and Francois-Louis. She cherished spending special days with her loved ones. Joannie always carefully selected gifts for the people she loved. She even enjoyed receiving presents herself. Joannie especially liked girly gifts, like perfume and jewelry.

In January Canada's best skaters descended upon Vancouver for the 2008 Canadian Championships. Joannie set her sights on winning a fourth straight title. The competition took place at the Pacific Coliseum, the same arena that would host the figure skating events at the 2010 Olympics.

"Every time we perform there, we can imagine the Olympic rings," Joannie told the *Canwest News Service*.

Joannie nearly landed a triple-triple combination in the short program but tumbled to the ice. The rest of her program went well and she placed first ahead of Mira Leung.

Organizers of the Canadian championships scheduled the ladies long program start time for 8:45 on a Sunday morning. The unusually early call time displeased the competitors.

"I'm not a morning person. I hate mornings," Joannie joked upon her arrival.

She left the ice with a smile, though, winning her fourth Canadian title. Mira held on for the silver medal and Cynthia Phaneuf took third.

Joannie next traveled to Korea for the Four Continents Championships. She skated very well, earning the silver medal. Mao Asada won the gold medal, while Miki Ando finished third.

"This competition gives me confidence," she told a pool of reporters.

One month later Joannie landed in Gothenburg, Sweden, for the 2008 World Championships. In the short program, she landed all her jumps cleanly for sixth place.

As Joannie left the arena, she turned to a pool of reporters.

"I want to get back into the top five," she said with determination.

Joannie had a blast skating to "Don Juan" in the long program. She landed five first-class triple jumps, including a triple toe loop-triple Salchow sequence. Joannie moved up to fifth place. She had accomplished her goal!

Meanwhile, Mao won her first world title. Carolina Kostner took silver, while Yuna Kim finished third.

"I'm happy with my season," Joannie said after the competition's conclusion.

The next day Joannie skated in the exhibition gala to George Gershwin's "Summertime." After her performance a few people remarked that Joannie looked so relaxed during her skate. They gushed that the lyrical music suited her perfectly. Some even commented that "Summertime" would make a great competitive program for her.

Next season's prep work had kicked into gear.

14

The Test Event

Joannie found an instrumental version of "Summertime" that world ice dancing champion Shae-Lynn Bourne choreographed as a competitive short program.

Joannie then fulfilled a lifelong dream of working with choreographer Lori Nichol for the long program. It became the most challenging, but rewarding, experience of her career.

Joannie and Lori brought Spanish composer Joaquín Rodrigo's popular classical guitar composition, "Concierto de Aranjuez," to life. Joannie felt excited and thrilled to skate to the music. She had long dreamed of using it as a program.

Lori was meticulous in her program creations. Every element, even jump entries and exits, served exact purposes in Lori's choreography. Joannie would spend a season performing the most difficult long program of her career.

Right before the season began, Joannie made two promises to herself. First, she would have fun with her skating. Second, she would have more confidence in herself.

At her first competition of the year, Joannie heard the Ottawa crowd roar as she skated onto the ice for the Skate Canada short program. For a second panic ran through her body. Joannie then reminded herself to channel her nerves into positive energy. Her body relaxed. She wanted to have fun while showing everyone how hard she worked during the off-season.

Joannie landed every jump in a breathtaking first-place performance. More importantly she enjoyed every second of her skate.

Joannie skated even better in the long program, taking her time with each element and using her body to tell a story. In the end she easily won the competition.

"Working with new choreographers, a psychologist, and a new team has really helped me," Joannie said happily.

Joannie arrived at Trophee Eric Bompard finally believing she could compete with skating's best. She needed such strong self confidence because she would square off against world champion Mao Asada, a woman she had never beaten.

In the short program Joannie emerged as the surprise leader despite falling on her triple flip-triple toe loop combination. Mao botched her combination as well, but unlike Joannie, she didn't maintain her focus throughout the rest of the program.

As Joannie walked to the boards to prepare for her long program, the crowd seemed unusually reserved. She realized that Mao, normally a huge crowd pleaser, must have had another difficult skate.

Manon did not want Joannie to concentrate too much on winning. She reminded her pupil to simply enjoy her skating and believe in herself.

Joannie delivered another great performance. The audience gave her a standing ovation, while the judges awarded her the gold medal!

After the competition reporters asked Joannie how it felt to beat Mao for the first time. The level-headed competitor managed to keep her victory in perspective.

"Being ahead of the world champion feels great, but both of us were not 100 percent tonight, so I'm focused on the rest of the season now," she said modestly.

An overachiever from a young age, Joannie often pushed herself too hard. When she returned home to train for the Grand Prix Final, she did not take time to rest after a whirlwind schedule. Instead Joannie threw herself into her college studies while she continued training at a high level.

One morning as Joannie raced to get ready for a busy day, she felt a sharp pain in her back. A pulled back muscle kept her off the ice for several days. She lost costly training time for the Grand Prix Final. Joannie realized that she had to stop overextending herself.

At the Grand Prix Final, Joannie delivered a disastrous short program. Although her long program went much better, she only moved up to fourth in the overall standings. Joannie viewed missing the podium with a mature observation.

"It gives me a wake-up call. I need to be better for the world championships," she told *The Province*.

At the 2009 Canadian Championships, Joannie's bid to retain her title hit a snag during the short program. She popped her double Axel and fell on the Lutz, finishing second behind Cynthia Phaneuf.

Before the long program Joannie warmed up backstage as cameras followed her intently. Some wondered if she would cave under the pressure.

When her music started Joannie remembered to have fun. She got lost in the emotion of her performance. The triple jumps came effortlessly, all seven of them, including a triple-triple sequence and back-to-back double Axels.

Four years earlier Joannie skated perhaps the greatest ladies long program at a Canadian championship. Now she managed to top her own greatness! The audience stood as one when her performance ended. Joannie burst into tears of joy.

"I'm not someone who usually expresses much at the end of my performance, but today I was really proud of myself," she later explained. "That's why I was so emotional."

Joannie won her fifth Canadian championship in dramatic fashion. A gracious Cynthia won the silver medal, and Amelie Lacoste placed third.

"I put myself in the toughest position I've ever had to skate," Joannie admitted to the press.

Talk of her medal chances at worlds inevitably resurfaced. After the emotional last 24 hours, Joannie believed she could accomplish anything now.

"This was the hardest test," she stated.

The next month a mini-preview of the 2010 Olympics played out at the Four Continents Championships. Vancouver used the competition to test out its figure skating venue in preparation for the world's largest stage.

Mao Asada, Yuna Kim, and Joannie headlined the ladies event. The wide talent pool would also offer a glimpse of how the upcoming world championships might turn out. A good showing by Joannie would boost her momentum as she headed into the big competition in Los Angeles.

A boisterous Vancouver crowd gathered to watch the ladies event. In the past such attention might have unnerved Joannie, but not anymore! She could hardly wait to compete for the enthusiastic audience!

Joannie skated a perfect short program, settling into second behind leader Yuna Kim, while Cynthia placed third.

"I tried to be more light and free and skate with more freedom," Joannie happily told the press. "It felt great to lay down a clean program before worlds."

Two days later Joannie delivered an equally strong long program. She took the silver medal behind winner Yuna. Mao roared back from sixth place to place third.

After the medal ceremony the three celebrated ladies gathered to pose for photographers. Flash bulbs went off everywhere. Fans shouted the medalists' names as they clamored for their attention. Officials waited nearby to usher the winners into the press conference room.

When Joannie left the ice, she gushed excitedly, "This competition had an Olympic feel!"

15
Los Angeles:
Where Dreams Come True

The sun shined brightly in Southern California on a Friday morning in March. At long last the 2009 World Championships had arrived. Hopefully Joannie would leave Los Angeles, the city of dreams, with a beautiful medal.

Fifty-four competitors had entered the ladies short program event. Skaters from countries as far away as Turkey and India filed into the Staples Center for a chance at the world title. With such a large competitive field, officials expected the short program to last over eight hours!

The ISU's world rankings determined the skate order. The higher the skater ranked, the later they skated in the day. Joannie would not take the ice until the late afternoon.

Joannie admired the beautiful weather as she left her hotel and headed towards the famous sports arena that also served as home to the NBA's Los Angeles Lakers. She felt great. Her practices had sailed along smoothly all week. She couldn't wait to skate her short program.

As Joannie waited by the rink boards moments before her short program, American Rachael Flatt had just just wrapped up her debut at the world championships. The California native had finished a strong short program right in front of her home state! The crowd went wild with applause for the diminutive blonde who lived just a short drive away. The teenager reacted with youthful enthusiasm as she waved to the crowd in excitement.

Now an experienced competitor with a veteran's mindset, Joannie vowed to use the crowd's energy to her advantage. She would not let the audience's enthusiasm rattle her. A world medal would not slip through her fingers again.

Joannie took a final sip from her water bottle and gave good luck hand slaps to Manon and Shae-Lynn. Her golden ponytail swished back and forth as she skated to her starting position.

For the last time the opening notes of "Summertime" played for the Canadian champion. Joannie looked the picture of composure as she began her program with a bright smile. She landed a perfect double Axel and then a triple Lutz-double toe loop combination. She flew through a combination spin and performed steps leading into a triple flip. Gorgeous! She had landed all her jumps perfectly! Manon and Shae-Lynn hugged each other in excitement!

Joannie skated so lightly it looked as if she floated on air. The crowd applauded appreciatively at her difficult footwork display and beautiful spirals. After a final layback spin, Joannie's performance ended. She bowed gracefully to a standing ovation.

When she sat down in the kiss and cry, Joannie blew kisses at the camera, while Manon beamed with pride. Joannie let out a deep breath while waiting nervously for her marks.

The scores were very strong! She and Manon exchanged joyful smiles. Joannie looked at Shae-Lynn as if to thank her.

At the end of the day, Joannie finished second behind Yuna Kim. Mao Asada placed third while Miki Ando took fourth. Joannie expressed delight with her performance and placement.

"I'm getting out of this building with a big smile," Joannie said proudly.

If the Canadian champion felt any nerves about the next day's final, they didn't show.

"I feel confident for the long program, and I'm anxious to come back tomorrow," she said excitedly.

The next evening the Staples crowd excitedly cheered for the final group of competitors. The three ladies who made the podium would spend the next year as Olympic medal favorites. The six women looked especially focused in the warm-up. They dodged each other's paths as cameras from all over the world followed their every move.

Joannie had a terrific warm-up. She looked loose and relaxed. She rotated her jumps effortlessly with controlled landings.

Incredibly, Tara Lipinski and Michelle Kwan sat in the stands as spectators just a few hundred feet away! Liz Manley, the last Canadian ladies skater to medal at the world championships, also sat nearby and cheered enthusiastically for the medal hopeful. For years Joannie had watched her idols skate. Now they watched her!

"The next competitor represents Canada," the arena announcer boomed. "Please give a warm welcome now for Joannie Rochette!"

Joannie exchanged familiar good luck hand slaps with Manon. Right off the bat she landed a triple Lutz-double toe-double loop and a beautiful triple flip. However, Joannie then missed the timing on her triple loop and doubled it. Refusing to let her mistake destroy her program, Joannie held onto her second triple Lutz. Then she landed a jump sequence no other woman in the competition attempted, a triple toe-triple Salchow sequence. She dazzled in her footwork and spiral sequences before landing back-to-back double Axels and a final triple Salchow. Her blurring combination spin signaled the end of her program. Many stood in admiration.

"Destiny is calling," Kurt Browning said on the CBC broadcast.

Moments later an emotional Joannie looked overwhelmed when her high marks appeared. It looked like her dream of standing on the world podium might finally come true. She placed her hands over her face and wept softly. A proud Francois-Louis sat smiling in the audience.

Yuna skated onto the ice a few moments later. From her opening triple flip-triple toe loop to her exquisite musical interpretation, she displayed a brilliant mix of jumping and artistry in her exciting "Scheherazade" routine. She slipped into first place easily.

As she sat in second place, Joannie waited backstage as competitor after competitor tried to pass her for a spot on the medal podium. Yet no one else could beat her. At the end of the competition, a thrilled Joannie finished in second place! At last her dream came true. She had won a world medal!

"This means so much to me," an emotional Joannie told the press. "Five years ago, I wouldn't have believed I could be here today. This year, I felt why not? It could be me. I've been training consistently all year. This is a dream come true."

When Joannie turned around, she found herself looking directly at Liz Manley, who offered a hearty congratulations! The two skaters embraced and then they shared a sweet conversation where they discussed their love for the color silver.

At the start of the medal ceremony, Joannie applauded as Yuna heard herself introduced as world champion for the first time. The emotional winner waved to the crowd and then climbed to the top step of the podium.

Then Joannie's turn to shine arrived. She took a deep breath as she waited to hear the magical worlds she had dreamed of for so long.

"Second and winner of the silver medal, representing Canada, Joannie Rochette!" the arena announcer proclaimed.

Joannie skated happily to center ice and bowed to the crowd. Next, she kissed Yuna on the cheek as they exchanged heartfelt congratulations.

Both skaters then clapped as bronze medalist Miki took her bows next. The three women had competed against each other for years.

Joannie smiled as Yuna accepted the gold medal. Then Joannie bowed her head as an official placed a silver medal around her neck. She picked up her precious souvenir in her delicate hands, studying it carefully. Then she applauded as Miki received her bronze medal.

Joannie watched proudly as officials raised the Canadian flag during the ceremony. Yuna sobbed as her country's national anthem filled the arena. She wiped her tears and looked bashfully at Joannie who smiled back at her with a knowing look. She could relate to Yuna's tearful reaction. She understood how emotional it felt to stand on the podium at the world championships.

16
Look Out, Vancouver

After winning the world silver medal, Joannie Rochette became one of Canada's top sports stars. She appeared on television talk shows, met Quebec Premier Jean Charest and received honors in a ceremony at the Legislature. She even walked the red carpet at the MuchMusic Video Awards.

Endorsement opportunities also rolled in. Joannie promoted hair products, drinks, a telecommunications company and cold medicine. She even appeared on General Mills' cereal boxes!

Joannie also continued touring with *Stars on Ice*, performing two solo performances, an upbeat number to Shakira's "Objection" and an inspirational routine to Suzie McNeil's "Believe." She even appeared in Suzie's music video for the song.

Joannie always made time for Francois-Louis. They enjoyed going for walks and planned hiking outings, too. Both even gained appreciation for one another's sports. A few times Francois-Louis took Joannie speed skating. She loved the sensation of flying fast on speed skates. When Joannie invited Francois-Louis to her rink one day, he tried a Lutz jump.

Joannie also saw her fan base grow even bigger. Fan clubs devoted to her popped up all over the Internet. Members lived as far away as Hong Kong, Switzerland, Panama and Austria!

Joannie understood how it felt to admire athletes. A long-time tennis fan, she had followed the sport from a young age. She loved watching tennis matches. If she couldn't watch a match in person, she would catch it on television. Of all the talented tennis players in the world, she most admired Spain's Rafael Nadal for his fighting spirit and great showmanship.

Joannie used her new fame to support causes she believed in, as well. She became a spokeswoman for World Vision Canada, a humanitarian group that improves living conditions for impoverished children around the world. On her first important mission, Joannie traveled to Peru and watched first-hand as World Vision gave families such needed items as chickens, cows and seeds so they could provide for their future. The experience made Joannie count her blessings. She suddenly felt silly for ever having whined over a bad practice when people had life threatening problems.

With the Vancouver Olympics months away, skating called to Joannie once more. She already knew which music she wanted to use for the Olympic season: "Samson and Delilah." Joannie had saved the music for a special season. She and Lori Nichol created a dramatic long program based on the famed biblical story.

Joannie then flew to Toronto to work with Shae-Lynn Bourne on her Olympic short program. They spent many long hours crafting the perfect tango routine.

Back in her home rink, Joannie laced up her skating boots. Once on the ice she took a deep breath and slowly warmed-up before practice. As always Manon stood nearby watching her carefully. That's exactly how Joannie wanted it.

In several months hundreds of cameras would follow Joannie's every move. Billions would watch as she chased her Olympic dream. Canada would hold its collective breath to see if Joannie could win a ladies figure skating medal for the home country.

Right in that moment, though, Joannie skated alone on the ice with only her Olympic dreams to keep her company. She finished her warm-up and skated to Manon.

The coach looked expectantly into her student's determined blue eyes.

"Ready?" Manon asked.

"Ready," Joannie replied.

Joannie Rochette

17
2010 Olympics: Tragedy & Triumph

The 2010 Vancouver Olympics began as a dream for Joannie. She proudly marched in the thrilling Opening Ceremonies and then moved into an apartment in the Olympic Village with ice dancer and pal Tessa Virtue. She felt excited, well trained and resolved to bring Canada its first Olympic figure skating ladies medal in 22 years. Joannie planned to enjoy every day of the Olympic Games.

Sadly, sometimes life does not go exactly as planned. As it turned out, the 2010 Olympics tested Joannie's emotional and physical strength like nothing she had ever experienced. It also catapulted her into the most talked about athlete at the Vancouver games—all before she ever skated her short program.

Normand and Therese Rochette landed in Vancouver on a Saturday morning, three days before the ladies short program. Family and friends accompanied the Rochettes on what should have been a joyous occasion—watching their beloved daughter compete in the world's most prestigious sporting event.

Upon their arrival Normand and Therese visited with Joannie. Afterwards, the couple went to dinner with some friends and then returned to an apartment they had rented in Vancouver.

At 6 a.m. the following day, Normand arrived alone at Joannie's room to deliver heartbreaking news to his daughter. Earlier that morning, Joannie's mother had suffered a fatal heart attack. Doctors had pronounced her dead at a Vancouver hospital.

Losing a parent is a difficult struggle to endure. Joannie was no exception. She and her mom shared a very close bond. They saw each other often and spoke on the phone every single day. Joannie felt devastated by her mother's death.

Joannie spent the morning grieving with her father. She also shared time with Manon, who was close to Therese and mourned her lost friend.

Skate Canada was immediately available to help Joannie through such a tough time. They offered her a grief counselor. Officials also assured her that she did not have to compete if it would be too difficult for her.

A devoted daughter, Joannie was tempted to forget about herself and care strictly for her father. Manon then spoke to Joannie as a coach. She reminded the skater that she was in Vancouver to pursue her dreams.

After a short deliberation, Joannie announced that she would compete in the Olympics. Her mom would want her to continue her Vancouver journey. She would pay tribute to her mother by competing in her honor. Normand told his daughter that he supported her decision wholeheartedly.

Mere hours after receiving the distressing news, Joannie arrived at Pacific Coliseum for her afternoon practice session. Word of the Rochettes' tragedy had quickly spread throughout the world. The other competitors were surprised to see Joannie at the practice, but they admired her determination.

Joannie's teammate Cynthia Phaneuf remarked, "I think she's doing the right thing. She's not going to feel better staying in her room. Joannie is a very courageous person and hats off that she is competing."

Normand sat in the practice stands surrounded by family and friends. On the worst day of his life, he would support his daughter through her most difficult practice ever.

Dressed in a simple cranberry tank top and black leggings, a tearful Joannie solemnly stepped onto the ice. As she wiped away tears spilling from her swollen red eyes, Joannie acknowledged her father with a small wave. Manon tried to keep the mood light by smiling a lot and remaining positive. Well-conditioned, Joannie had a very strong program run-through. She then returned to her room at the Olympic Village where she continued to mourn the loss of her mother.

Surprisingly, Joannie found solace in the form of her iPhone. Days earlier she had skated an especially strong practice session. Joannie was so excited that she phoned her mother to relay the good news. Therese later returned Joannie's call and left a voice mail telling her daughter how proud she was of her. "I know you'll be on the podium," Therese had said. Joannie had saved that message. When she listened to it again, it brought her comfort.

An outpouring of support immediately reached Canada's ladies champion. Joannie received letters, phone calls and emails from people all over the world. Everyone, from celebrities like

Celine Dion and Olympic champion Dan Jansen, to everyday folks, contacted Joannie to express their sympathy for her loss.

The media was naturally curious to see how Joannie would handle her struggle. News outlets from all over the globe clamored to talk to the Olympian.

Joannie politely declined all interview requests, though. Skate Canada also asked people to respect their skater's privacy. Joannie felt determined to skate well for her mother, and she did not want any distractions getting in the way of her goal.

On a rainy Tuesday evening, the world's eyes fixated on Joannie as the ladies competition got underway with the short program. Thirty competitors rounded out the event. Joannie would skate first in the final group.

Prior to leaving for the competition, Joannie listened to her mother's final voice mail again. She knew that her mom's words would inspire her.

When the arena announcer asked the five ladies to take the ice for their warm-up, the crowd stood when he called Joannie's name. They acknowledged the courage she had shown during the past few days.

Joannie wiped her eyes as she circled the ice and practiced her jumps. The audience cheered loudly for every move and cameras filmed every breath she took.

When the competitors were asked to leave the ice, Joannie skated over to Manon. Her eyes still brimming with tears, she listened to her coach's valuable advice. Then they exchanged their familiar good luck hand slaps. Finally the determined athlete skated to her start position at center ice.

Everyone in the arena and those watching at home seemed to hold their collective breath for Joannie. Tango music filled the arena. After a four-year wait, Joannie's Olympic competition had finally begun.

Joannie gathered speed for her first jump combination—the triple Lutz-double toe. She needed to land it perfectly to vault into medal contention. The crowd cheered as she nailed the combination. Her second jump, the triple flip, was also crucial. Joannie skated to the other side of the rink in a series of difficult steps, launched into the air, rotated three times and came down confidently on her blade. A gorgeous double Axel completed her jump requirements. The audience roared for their countrywoman. When her music ended, Joannie shed a fresh set of tears as the crowd showered her with a standing ovation.

"I felt a lot of love from the crowd," Joannie later commented. "It was very emotional to get so much love in one moment."

She hadn't just survived the most grueling program she'd ever have to deliver; she had also given the performance of her career. Joannie skated over to Manon and hugged her tightly as she sobbed with relief.

Joannie's gutsy short program performance quickly became the stuff of Olympic legend. People everywhere marveled at the courageous young woman who had overcome heartbreak to deliver perfection on the world's biggest stage. By the next morning

Joannie found herself on the front page of newspapers all over the world.

The judges were also impressed with Joannie's performance. She earned a season best score of 71.36 and settled into third place behind leader Yuna Kim and second place finisher Mao Asada.

Afterwards, Joannie politely declined to speak with the press. She instead issued a statement through Skate Canada. "It was hard to handle, but I appreciate the support," she said simply.

Joannie drew to skate second to last in the final group for the long program two days later. She arrived at Pacific Coliseum a couple of hours before her start time. Manon watched carefully as Joannie stretched backstage. Olympic organizers had reserved a quiet room for Joannie so she could prepare for her performance without intrusive cameras filming her every move. She also wanted to avoid interaction with anyone. Over the past few days, Joannie had dissolved into tears whenever anyone would look at her with sad eyes. She needed to maintain her composure in order to skate a strong long program.

American Rachael Flatt led off the final group with a strong jumping display. Japan's Miki Ando followed with an equally solid performance.

Yuna Kim took the ice next, delivering a superb athletic and artistic performance that earned her record-setting marks. Mao Asada followed with a strong performance of her own by landing two triple Axels in her program.

Joannie knew when the announcer called her name that every woman in her group had delivered excellent programs. She had to skate equally well if she wanted to remain in the top three and secure a medal.

Joannie skated to her start position. She would summon all her physical and mental strength to fulfill her promise.

For four minutes Joannie shut out life's distractions and concentrated on skating her *Samson and Delilah* program, as she practiced it nearly every day. She skated beautifully, landing several triple jumps including her dazzlingly triple-triple sequence. The adoring audience gave her another standing ovation as they showered her with applause. As Joannie finished she blew a kiss to her father who cheered her on in the stands. Then she blew another kiss, this time skyward, to acknowledge her mother.

Joannie easily won the bronze medal. She had accomplished a lifelong goal. When Joannie stepped onto the medal podium, she smiled bravely through tears as the precious medal hung from her neck.

After the awards ceremony, Joannie draped Canada's flag around her shoulders and circled the rink to the roar of her home country. When she came off the ice, Normand waited for her by the boards. Father and daughter embraced for a moment. Normand then managed a smile as he held Joannie's medal in his hands and kissed it.

The grace, composure and strength with which Joannie handled her heartbreak turned her into a worldwide superstar. She became the face of the Vancouver Olympics and a symbol of courage and triumph under tragedy.

Joannie also became the co-recipient of the inaugural Terry Fox Award introduced at the Vancouver Olympics. The honor went to the individual who displayed courage, humility and extraordinary athletic abilities at the 2010 Winter Games.

"I didn't plan on inspiring so many people," Joannie said modestly, when she learned of her achievement. "I know my mom is up there watching and is so proud."

On the final day of the Vancouver Olympics, Joannie received the greatest honor of her career. She was selected to carry the flag for Canada in the Closing Ceremonies. Joannie reacted to the news with her usual humility.

"Why me?" she asked smiling shyly. "It has been a tough week for me, but I am going to walk into that stadium with a big smile on my face."

As the Olympics wrapped up, Joannie's thoughts lingered on two subjects dear to her heart—her mother and figure skating.

"I just wanted to try and have no regrets ten years from now," she remarked. "I think that's what my mom would have wanted me to do—to go after my dreams."

A
About the Authors

Christine Dzidrums holds a bachelor's degree in Theater Arts from California State University, Fullerton. She served as editor-in-chief of *Ice Skating Magazine* for several years. Christine recently completed two young adults novels, *Cutters Don't Cry* and *Kaylee: The What If Game.* She is working on her third book entitled, *Your Friend, Ashleigh.*

Leah Rendon graduated with a Bachelor of Arts degree from the University of California, Los Angeles. Throughout her writing career she has covered major skating events, including the Winter Olympic Games, the Grand Prix Series and the World Figure Skating Championships. She has also interviewed many top athletes, including Olympic champions Katarina Witt, Brian Boitano and Oksana Baiul.

Joannie Rochette

B
Results

SENIOR LEVEL

2010 Winter Olympics - 3
2010 Canadian Championships - 1
2009 ISU Grand Prix Final - 5
2009 Skate Canada - 1
2009 Cup of China - 3
2009 Japan Open - 1
2009 World Championships - 2
2009 Four Continents - 2
2009 Canadian Championships - 1
2008 ISU Grand Prix Final - 4
2008 Trophee Eric Bompard - 1
2008 Skate Canada - 1
2008 World Championships - 5
2008 Four Continents - 2
2008 Canadian Championships - 1
2007 Cup of Russia - 3
2007 Skate Canada - 3
2007 World Championships - 10
2007 Four Continents - 3
2007 Canadian Championships - 1
2006 Trophee Eric Bompard - 4
2006 Skate Canada - 1
2006 World Championships - 7
2006 Winter Olympics - 5

2006 Canadian Championships - 1
2005 Trophee Eric Bompard - 4
2005 Skate Canada - 2
2005 Canadian Championships - 1
2004 ISU Grand Prix Final - 3
2004 Trophee Eric Bompard - 1
2004 Cup of China - 3
2004 World Championships - 8
2004 Four Continents - 4
2004 Canadian Championships - 2
2003 Cup of Russia - 4
2003 Bofrost Cup on Ice - 1
2003 Skate Canada - 10
2003 World Championships - 17
2003 Four Continents - 8
2003 Canadian Championships - 2
2002 Four Continents - 9
2002 Canadian Championships - 3

Junior Level

2002 World Junior Championships - 5
2001 Jr. Grand Prix Italy - 3
2001 Jr. Grand Prix Poland - 5
2001 World Junior Championships - 8
2001 Canadian Championships - 1st
2000 Jr. Grand Prix Mexico - 4
2000 Jr. Grand Prix France - 5

Novice Level

2000 Canadian Championships - 1
2000 North American Challenge Skate - 1
2000 Mladost Trophy - 1
1999 Canadian Championships - 15

C
Links

Skate Canada's Official Website:
WWW.SKATECANADA.CA

Joannie Rochette's Official Website:
WWW.JOANNIEROCHETTE.COM

Skating Photography:
WWW.JBARRYMITTAN.COM

Skating Photography:
WWW.JAYADEFF.COM

Book Information at:
WWW.CANADIANICEPRINCESS.COM

Author Information:
WWW.CHRISTINEDZIDRUMS.COM

Stars on Ice:
WWW.STARSONICE.COM

World Vision:
WWW.WVI.ORG/WVI/WVIWEB.NSF

Made in the USA
Middletown, DE
16 December 2014